DAVID KING
MAN OF STEAM

Bygones presented by Anglia Television

DAVID KING
MAN OF STEAM

Talking to Dick Joice

The Boydell Press · Ipswich

Published by The Boydell Press Ltd
PO Box 24 Ipswich IP1 1JJ

ISBN 0 85115 103 5

Photoset and printed in Great Britain by
Lowe & Brydone Printers Limited, Thetford, Norfolk

FOREWORD

I have listened to innumerable people since I first started in television twenty years ago. It was put to me in the early days that a good interviewer only needed to ask the initial question with an occasional supplementary to keep the interviewee going and that an interviewer did not need to be an expert in the subject. In fact, it is probably better if he is merely an "informed idiot" on most subjects.

David King told me the greater part of his story sitting in the comfortable chairs in his "Engineerium" (rear cover). I must explain that this is an old railway guard's van that he has fitted up with a boiler – steam of course – which is in turn connected by copper pipes to about twelve small steam engines, some of which were built by him and some collector's pieces! It is here that David sits when he wants to relax and think to the quiet "chuff" of the little engines and the very distinctive "scent" of steam and oil.

With David King it isn't difficult to become an enthusiast – if not an expert – certainly on the subject of steam for he is a marvellous raconteur. Listening to him made me realise that there was much more to the man than enthusiasm and a great deal of knowledge, for he has developed a way of life that I feel is well worth recording. He has achieved what many of us realise too late in life and that is, as he would say, "You want to make haste slowly for you get there just as fast".

I hope in writing his story I have captured something of him. If I have I hope some of his words will rub off on you as they did on me. It has been great fun to read, record, transcribe and edit what I think *is* David King – Man of Steam.

DICK JOICE

It's not surprising that I'm a mechanically minded chap, for all my forebears seem to have been. I remember going to stay with an elderly relative when I was a boy and, finding a mechanical vegetable cutter in his cellar, had high hopes of it being given to me. But no, although I'm sure he hadn't come across it for years, he soaked it in paraffin, cleaned it up and as far as I know it hasn't been seen since!

One of the last things my maternal grandfather did in 1940 when he was 82 was to get up a ladder and take down the sign bearing the name of the road and rip off the sign giving the name of his house in order to confuse the Germans if they invaded this country. He also pumped up the family tricycle in order that he might, together with the rest of the family, as he said, make a dignified retreat if necessary.

It was in that household at Barford in Norfolk that he and my grandmother launched their family of four on an unsuspecting world. One of the family went to America in a hurry with her boy friend and came back married and pregnant even quicker. Grandad's reaction to that – "She could have stopped at home and done it – it would have been cheaper."

The other side of the family, the Kings, were millers at Wymondham for goodness only knows how far back, certainly to the early 1800s. Their mill, the North Mill, was a beautiful piece of wind-driven machinery and had quite a history. Called the "much travelled mill" because it was originally built in Lincolnshire and was moved to Norfolk bit by bit, it had an octagonal tower and was dismantled by sawing the corner posts "by hand" from top to bottom – a daunting task even today. The whole thing was then re-erected at Ludham and owned by an uncle of my grandfather. When this uncle died, grandfather decided to "up sticks" or rather "up mill" again and move it to its final resting place at Wymondham, 30 miles away. Not only did he move it but he heightened it as well by building the whole thing on a 14 feet high brick plinth. He used to say: "There's a lot more wind to use the higher up you go." It was by far the highest mill in the county and was magnificent in its stark livery of black and white.

But my Father was not so mill minded. What he really liked was steam. About the turn of the century he built a steam-driven dynamo to generate electricity, the first in Wymondham. It was 110 volts as opposed to the mains which were and still are 250 volts. In fact his premises were never connected to the mains as he always maintained that such a high voltage is not safe. The fact that the low voltage put the installation outside the Factory Act may have had some bearing on his opinion. In the same vein they had a small wind-driven bandsaw which worked quite satisfactorily and safely for seventy years and then along came a Factory Inspector and condemned it as unsafe. Still, no doubt the Inspector was only doing his job – and earning his money, though that wasn't how Father saw it.

About the turn of the century Father became more interested in saw milling and dealing in timber, in fact a pit saw had been in use at the Northfield Mill site for some time. Eventually a four-acre field, complete

The 'much travelled mill' at Wymondham c. 1900

with turnips, was bought on the other side of the town, bounded by the London and North Eastern Railway to the east and the Browick Road to the north. This field became the site of the railway works, and the home of Alfred King and Son, Timber Merchants. The Northfield Mill was sold for £500 complete with miller's house and cottages. Those were the days.

Railway Works was off to a good start, usable sand for concrete was on the site, or under it, they only had to dig it up. Timber-framed buildings were erected to house the bandsaw, driven now from a portable steam engine, and all the other things like drying sheds that go to make up a saw mill. Timber was brought in by our own steam tractors, and a ready market was found for our hardwood. A water supply was a problem to start with, everyone assuring Father that no water could possibly be found on the site. However, it would take more than a little pessimism from the locals to put Father off, so a borehole was sunk to a considerable depth without finding water. Despair set in. It was decided that at least the pipe could be salvaged, so a 100-ton jack was brought in to pull it out of the ground again. Upon lifting the pipe a few feet an abundant supply of the precious liquid was found! And that bore has never been known to dry up to this day.

The advent of the first war seemed to assure a never ending demand for timber, so the saw mill expanded. Nearly every manufacturing concern in the country became involved in the supply of war materials with the resulting disastrous void when peace was declared, and the outlets for immense tonnages of materials dried up almost overnight. We had no choice but to find an alternative outlet for our timber, and various products were made on the premises. Batches of farm gates were turned out, and one of these was still to be seen at Forncett St. Mary nearly 40 years later. Eventually the idea of building furniture was settled upon after several attempts most of which ended up on the local saleground! The firm gradually settled into cabinet making and furniture manufacturing, after a great deal of hard and disheartening work by Father selling in London. I have heard him tell many times of the queues of salesmen outside the offices of buyers in the big London stores, only to be turned away without an interview even. Weekly trips to the big cities and persistence paid off and our goods gradually became accepted. King tables, which were our speciality, became well known for good quality. In the mid-Twenties Father decided to drop the timber felling and haulage side of the business, so we had an auction and sold off the traction engines and gear. Thereafter, all our timber was bought "at the stump" and delivered into the yard where it was unloaded by steam crane and left to weather for at least a year before being brought into the sawmill. After sawing into boards and planks, the timber was stacked again in the yard with 1 inch splines between each board for seasoning by air circulation, and there remained for another six to twelve months. The next process was to select and re-saw the wood into required sizes and then it was stacked in the kiln for two weeks, one with the steam on and one to cool off. I have heard Father say that a table leg 6 inches square could lose a gallon of water in those two weeks.

I arrived on the scene on the 28th August, 1932, which event was greeted with disgust, dismay, surprise or amusement depending on the status of the observer. My nearest brother was 14 at the time, so I cannot claim to be the result of planned parenthood. For some reason Father took to me more than the others, although I think he tried over the years to be fair to us all, but in different ways. We were living in Yarmouth at the time, and Father was commuting to Wymondham each day by train – thirty miles. About 1935 Father got fed up with journeying to and fro from Great Yarmouth and built a house on the site of the Railway Works. Planning permission was a mere formality to be treated lightly in those days. You built whatever was required and then casually mentioned this to the local council afterwards. Father usually did things not because that was the way they had always been done, but because that was the way that he thought was best and never mind tradition. A concrete-walled rectangle grew, enclosing two enormous rooms separated by an equally large hall. No doubt Father saw the function of the ground floor as somewhere to enter the dwelling, somewhere to eat and somewhere to relax – and what more could you want. The walls having reached the bedroom floor level, beams were laid across, not on edge as is usual, but flat. The upper floors overhung the base walls, and in later life the ends of the beams which supported the weight of the upper walls developed a disturbing sag. I often speculated on the prospect of opening the back door one day and finding that I was looking out of the upstairs bathroom window, the upper floor having telescoped to the ground. However, all credit to the designer, this has yet to happen. The interior was lined in a much simpler way than employing plasterers – sheets of plywood were simply nailed to the concrete. I must say that house turned out much better than everyone thought, except Father, who was ever critical of his own. Actually some of the interior woodwork was rather splendid, and was featured in one of the woodworking trade magazines of the time. The roof was surmounted with an observation platform, upon which it was suggested it would be pleasant to take tea. However, the tea-making authorities had other ideas and such an event never took place. Two enormous water tanks were in the loft, and these were filled up by pump from the bore, which led to an amusing incident. The tanks were open-topped and Father was disquieted to find the odd bird and other unwelcome wildlife terminating their stay in a watery grave. The tanks were consequently covered with two sheets of plywood, thus preserving the contents in a state fit for human consumption. The snag was that one day the delivery pipe from the pump discharged not into the tank but on to the plywood cover and, of course, Walter – whose job it was to pump up – duly set the machinery in motion ignorant of this fact. It takes some time for water delivered by pump to the top of the house to percolate down through the bedroom ceilings, through the bedding, through the bedroom floors, into the kitchen, lounge and hall and out of the front door. I am glad to say that although he got the blame Walter was with us many years. The house had another novel feature – a cold store. The idea was that underground the temperature is stable, a fact not overlooked by cellar builders of long ago. However, Father reasoned that it was only necessary for the food to be despatched underground and not the cook. So a dry well was sunk in the pantry and a crane-like lift lowered milk, butter and the like to the depths for inexpensive preservation. The unsuspected snag was that all sorts of small unwelcome creatures soon cottoned on and arrived by lift to the kitchen with our food.

During the construction of the house an unfortunate incident occurred. In a bad thunderstorm one of the workmen was standing in the doorway and was struck by lightning and instantly killed. Father was not superstitious, but he did voice the opinion that the house was unlucky. Looking back, how right he was. Our lives might have been very different had he given up building there, for in due course we moved in, and within two years Mother and Father had split up. After living with friends and relations, a week here and a week there, Mother and I ended up at Caister-on-Sea in 1938. A year later Adolf H. started on the rampage, which made it uncomfortable for those living on the East Coast, and those who could move inland were advised to do so. So it was "up sticks" for Mum and I again and off to Barford to live with the grandparents. I remember this little village attracting the attention of the Luftwaffe one night. This was mostly due to a bomb falling on a high tension pole which struck a passing petrol bowser, thus causing an interesting conflagration, rather than any deliberate plan to obliterate Barford. Anyway, having started trouble at what was obviously a strategic target, the enemy aircraft decided to give it the full treatment. Our family sought refuge under the dining table, a magnificent mahogany structure well able to withstand anything Hitler might send down. In the end very little damage took place, most of the bombs losing their force in the soft earth. I went with the other village lads the following day hunting for souvenirs. How I wish I had kept mine, but I sold it to a sightseer.

Soon Mother heard of a vacancy for a cook at the Hall in a nearby village. She took the post, and found some kind folk to look after me on a nearby farm. This was splendid but I got mumps and the "push" from my new digs and back we went to Wymondham, this time to a charming little cottage, the residence of a splendid soul, Nurse Read – a midwife. I can only look back on my mumps with pleasure. What a cosy little cottage that was, two up and two down, or was it one-and-a-half. I remember the stairs rose almost vertically from what seemed to be a cupboard beside the fireplace. The floors upstairs were so uneven that the point of arrival at the top was difficult to determine. Our lights were oil, of course. How much more natural than electricity. Why do we now need a hundred watts to do what would have been done by the light of five candle power? Father once showed me a beautiful piece of inlaid woodwork he had done when he was a lad, all by the light of a hurricane lamp after a day's work in the mill.

After completing the process of having mumps, the time came for us to move again. This time we moved into a bungalow with the wife and small son of one of the local grocers who had been called away to help deal with Hitler and his wife left to run the shop. There followed another pleasant interlude of a year or so, marred only for me by collecting a dose of osteomyelitis in my left index finger. I do not think I have ever had pain before or since like that.

The 'Unusual House' at Wymondham

It all started by a cut from a baked bean tin, which turned out to be not as hygienic as it looked. After a time the finger began to swell and fester, and eventually had to be lanced. This was all done at home, the medical profession did not have much time for small boys with cut fingers in those days of adult bloodshed. In the fullness of time it healed but the joint remained rigid, and the surgeon said "Now we'll cut it off" and Mother said "Not on your life". So he didn't. Good old Mum, she was usually right. Come to think of it, I've always had finger trouble. My right index finger I nearly lost after a little difference of opinion with a planing machine. This was after I had been working at Railway Works for about a couple of years. I was in hospital after having the wound repaired, and Father came along to the ward and told me that the surgeon was not satisfied and would have another go and that when I awoke my finger would probably be in the dustbin. No one thought of asking me, after all the only contribution I had made was to spend eighteen years growing the thing. Being under age Father had to give his permission for the anaesthetic – he wouldn't. But for him I should have lost that one too. I am glad to say, therefore, that whatever else I have lost over the years I still have ten fingers. I always did like to keep things in sets.

Whilst living in Tuttles Lane, Wymondham, I went to Lyndhurst School, where I suppose I must have learned something, but I am unable to remember just what. Eventually the time came for me to leave to continue my education on a higher plane, at least I presume that was the reason. I next remember sitting in a formidable academic atmosphere with some sort of examination paper. I think the idea was that if I could reach a certain level of achievement it would save Father a lot of money, but I rather think he was out of pocket on that one.

I was thus entrusted to the Tender Loving Care of the Headmaster and staff of Thetford Grammar School, whilst living initially at the Red Lion Public House, where Mum earned her keep for a time with Mr. and Mrs. Mills and family. They, like so many, showed us great kindness. A housekeeping post became vacant a short distance away, and we were soon installed with Mr. and Mrs. Parry, he being the manager of one of the maltings. What a splendid place for roller skating – vast areas of floor with only rows of posts in the way. The Parrys were an elderly couple with one son, who used to build model aeroplanes and photograph them for the Air Ministry for recognition training. Mrs. Parry had an air of great dignity, one of a class of fast dying aristocracy used to having servants and now reduced to doing a great deal for herself – with Mum's help of course. For me, one of the most endearing features of the maltings was a beautifully polished gas engine. I suppose it was about twenty horsepower. I can hear the gentle chuff now, and see the glint of the polished camshaft and blur of the crank. All long since gone I'm afraid, no doubt replaced by a grubby electric motor the size of a pail and doing the same job a thousand times more efficiently, blast it!

Mr. Parry was kind enough to let me have a room for a workshop at the Maltings, and this is where I used to leave my brain when I went to school. My teachers and I, with a few exceptions, were totally disinterested in one another, and as long as I kept my inability to learn by their methods from embarrassing them, they used to let my body quietly exist in the classroom. For some reason even now I cannot learn by conventional methods. If I attend a lecture on a subject that is of passionate interest to me, my mind cannot pay attention for more than a few minutes – about every sixty seconds I realise I have heard nothing of what has been said in the last 45 and have to wrench my attention back on to the subject. The experts, that is the few who took any notice, put my abysmal performance down to being a late and slow developer. I remember just before the School Certificate exam, the headmaster came into the class one day in order to review each individual boy's chances and to give a little advice, such as if George could start learning his tables and drag his mind away from the girls' school opposite he might avoid being expelled before the end of term. Then he came to me: "Ah, King" he said, "Yes, King, well him. Well, that's hard luck on King". Looking back I wouldn't change my luck for some of the lads who did pass their School Cert!

About 1943 somebody died on the Croxton Road and a little terraced house came on the market. I think Father paid about £400 for that and so for the first time since Caister in 1939 Mum and I had our own home again. I have some of my happiest memories there. We had a nice little house; two rooms downstairs, plus kitchen, upstairs there were two bedrooms, with a third tiny room made into a bathroom. A degree of modesty was achieved by sticky paper on the window. The method for heating the water was equally primitive.

We had some lovely neighbours. On one side was a dear old soul from Yorkshire, and her schoolteacher daughter with whom I used to play draughts. The manager of the local drapers and his wife lived on the other side. Down the road lived the town clerk. I used to be fascinated by his appearance. He looked to me just like a skeleton covered with light brown paper. He could have made a fortune in a medical school . . . a real living twelve-inch-to-the-foot-scale, working skeleton of homo sapiens. A kind man.

The most important feature of No. 49 Croxton Road, was a splendid garden shed, my workshop. I transplanted my brain there from the Maltings, where it would await, impatiently, my return from school each day. Even when I was quite small Father would buy me tools, most of which I still have today, which meant my workshop was fairly well equipped. He used to visit me each Saturday afternoon. I nearly always had a list of materials required for the following week. He never set foot in the house, drawing up outside and announcing his arrival by the car horn, which caused a flurry of curtains. I always felt embarrassed as there must have been much speculation amongst the local inhabitants about this car arriving once a week, especially at that time of petrol rationing.

Twenty-five years later I still have a great affection for the grey flint town of Thetford, which is set amongst some of the most enjoyable Norfolk countryside. I say enjoyable because not only has it a warm friendly feeling, but one can get amongst and become part of the pine trees, the bracken and the fine sweet grass. In Breckland, the soil having less agricultural value than some other places is left for Nature to do its best without interference – and Nature has been at it longer than mankind – but mankind nevertheless is made welcome. Even the vast Thetford Chase pine forest has blended with the scene and become complementary with another dimension and has an atmosphere of its own. The resinous tang in the air on a hot summer's day and the soft spring of pine needles underfoot make entering the forest more like stepping through the looking glass into another world. The Little Ouse river winds its charming way to Brandon and provides some of the best places for messing about in boats, camping and picnicking. The little villages of Santon, Two Mile Bottom and St. Helen's Well, all connected by dirt tracks, are places where one can stand back and look at life in its simplest terms and wonder at the good things which are free and which many do not value highly enough. Basically man needs to feed himself, keep warm and dry and see that those around him can do the same. All the rest of our modern whirlpool of possessions, position and push is so much ensnaring embellishment that robs us of contentment, which is truly what we all seek. Human nature pushes us forwards to seek this goal, which is all the time just behind us – it is only necessary to stand still and it will catch us up.

Still, I run on, so back to school. After the first year or two the staff became accustomed to my shortcomings – our history master being about the only one who realised that I might have some small spark of talent outside the sphere of life they had to offer. I remember him showing this by one day asking me to write an essay on "The Internal Combustion Engine". What a break! I tackled that with relish, and words flowed from my pen in a delicious torrent. I remember getting a mark of 85 out of 100. Unprecedented heights of achievement! I cannot say what that meant to someone used to marks of 4 out of 100 as the norm. I was no better with compulsory sport. I wonder who thought to call it sport, more like physical and mental torture to me. Still we had a choice – football in the winter and cricket in the summer – or was it the other way round. Rather like the choice of colours for Henry Ford's early cars – any colour you like as long as it was black!

In common with most schoolteachers, our English master had his strange ways. His speciality was to turn round common sayings, like "Too few cooks spoiled the broth", or, "He who hesitates is far from lost". He had a point, and I must admit that these sayings are very often just as true in reverse gear as the way round the authors intended. One such saying which applied to me in my early days was that it was better to "do something badly than not at all". I lived up to that in my workshop, turning out the most atrocious things. The trouble was that my hands could not keep up with my mind so everything was sacrificed in the name of speed. It took many years for my brain and hands to come to some sort of agreement so that speed of operation could be regulated to our mutual advantage. However, I did manage to turn out a continual stream of gadgets and models of all sorts. I vividly remember one device purporting to be a siren which I fitted to the front of my bike. This was driven from the front wheel and kept out of operation by a doubtful catch, very susceptible to jolts, which frequently brought the device into unannounced full screech. One Sunday afternoon, I was late for a church function which was to be blessed with my presence as a choir boy. I arrived at the church gates at some considerable speed, not unusual either in velocity or degree of lateness. Outside the gate there was a high curb to be negotiated which I did with considerable skill. However, the jolt set the siren into action simultaneously with my precipitation into the middle of the vicar and choir who happened to be assembled just inside the gates. I can still see the scattering of figures and surplices, all dignity gone to the wind. Our clergyman used to proudly boast that his choir was unpaid whereas the other churches in the town had to entice the schoolboys there with money. I think I preferred to keep a degree of freedom, whereby lateness or non-attendance could not result in loss of earnings.

I don't know why I was in the choir, I cannot say I enjoyed it very much for it meant being clean when I could be in my shed or missing something on the radio like "Itma" or "Much Binding in the Marsh". Talking about the wireless I think we used to enjoy the programmes on the radio far more than today's children enjoy television. At least we used to know what it was all about. Nowadays I often come in during a programme on the "box" and ask the family what is on and they have no idea of the title or the plot. The brain seems to become short-circuited somehow. The image goes into the eyes and then gets lost. Perhaps it runs out somewhere. Good job too. The thought of all that drivel actually going into millions of human brains all over the world fills me with foreboding. If there are beings in outer space picking up our television programmes, well, I don't wonder they have never bothered to land here.

How I survived some of my experiments in my shed is a mystery. I used to do the most suicidal things with mains electricity. There was no current supply when we moved to Croxton Road, so with the aid of some army telephone wire found by the roadside I soon had light and power. This wire was partly steel, so with any load was liable to heat up and even become red hot. That and the doubtful insulation was lethal enough, but what went on in the shed puts those dangers in the shade. What grandfather would have said I cannot imagine. He would never have mains electricity in his house at all. You see, I found that mains current was the ideal detonator for gunpowder. All one had to do was ram a suitable container full of the explosive and pass a piece of fuse wire through it. I used to bury this lot in the garden and arrange for the fuse wire to be blown by the mains through a time switch, which gave me time to retreat indoors and watch the results through the window. Luckily, no one visited us at one of these delicate moments! We used to have problems getting the saltpetre for gunpowder sometimes. There was one chemist who would oblige and even gave us advice on achieving the greatest devastation. Then he went out of business so we had to rely on an adult who could give a good excuse for wanting saltpetre. The usual excuse was to clean the chimney. A good way of sweeping chimneys was to throw a handful of explosive tightly wrapped in paper on the fire in a stove, copper or oven. The door of the fire was then slammed shut and secured with a broom handle whilst everyone retired to await the explosion! One of our pals was a signalman on the railway. It is surprising how frequently those signal box chimneys needed cleaning, especially in early November round about the fifth!

Another activity which has left me with many pleasant and worthwhile memories was the time I spent in the Boy Scouts. Our meetings took place in one of the many old Maltings to be found in Thetford. We senior scouts used an upstairs room and the juniors had the room underneath. In the absence of the seniors some of the younger ones used to venture into the sacred domain above and one day we thought we would teach them a lesson. The stairs led into a sort of porch as the upper room was lofty, and this porch had a ceiling of its own. Upon this ceiling we perched a board with a rope attached – the rope dangled down to the floor below. We then collected all the rubbish and floor sweepings that could be found and piled this on the board. A notice fixed to the rope which said DO NOT PULL was sufficient to ensure that some unsuspecting junior would give the rope a yank, and this is exactly what happened much to our extreme merriment and delight. The trouble was that one day the Cub Master was equally curious!

Our Scoutmaster was a splendid fellow. He was very seldom around and we used to run ourselves. I must say that looking back we were very orderly and well behaved, but that did not stop us having a jolly good time. Various items of camping gear were made, and I soon had a circular saw and other essential items running. Trailers for our gear were a favourite construction, using two bicycle wheels. It was the shortage of wheels which brought about the design of a sidecar which was highly successful as, of course, it only needed one wheel. Most weekends we would be off to our favourite camping site on the river; funny how the weather always seemed to be warm then. I cannot ever remember it raining, but maybe we did not notice such things. Our scoutmaster did visit us once or twice. He used to ride a little two-stroke motor bike. I think it was a Francis Barnet, or affectionately known as Fanny B. One year we had a long summer camp at Oulton Broad in the grounds of a large hall. We were taken by lorry and left to our own devices for a couple of weeks with the F.B. popping up once or twice to cast a fatherly eye upon his charges. About the worst thing to happen was that a friend and I had our money stolen from the changing rooms at the swimming pool. I remember thirty bob (£1.50) was involved. In those days the whole troop could dine out on that sum. However, that did not mar our holiday. We had little use for cash as long as there was stew to be cooked over the fire. I suppose now they've got gas stoves. I shall never forget the howls of derision that arose from our troop when we observed a rival organisation arriving at camp by lorry complete with iron bedsteads!

Another memorable camp took place at Sandringham, where there was a Scout Jamboree attended by chaps from all over the world. Two things stand out. One was a tin of hair oil which melted in the sun and ran into my sleeping bag, and the other was a gate which I constructed using our hand cart on its side and the wheels as a hinge. At least we had the only gate on site which swung on ball bearings! This camp, unfortunately, only lasted for a Whit weekend, but it is a memory I shall never forget. His Majesty, the King, sent a message to us all, regretting that he could not attend. I remember being very impressed that he should think of us.

By now I was in my last year at school and it became evident that all was not well. I began to lose weight and found I could not lift myself on the wall-bars in the gym, and most of all I developed a thirst which seemed insatiable. No matter how much I drank it made no difference – six cups of tea with every meal and two or three glasses of water before returning to school and getting up all night drinking. Mother had an idea what was wrong as she had had a distant aunt who used to take a bedroom ewer to her room at night full of lemonade and in the morning it would all be gone. That must have been at least two gallons. So one Saturday evening we visited our family G.P. and he soon confirmed Mother's suspicions that I was diabetic. I had no idea what that meant, but looking back Mother must have gone through a distressing time. The following Wednesday I was admitted to The West Suffolk Hospital under Dr. Joyce Cochran, one of God's gifts to mankind. What a kind, considerate and generous soul she was. I certainly owe in no small measure my well being of the last 30 years to her skill. My spell in the Maitland Wilson Ward I can only look upon with pleasure. It was Christmas and the other patients were a happy crowd. My fingers soon started to itch for some creative work and with the help and generosity of a dear old boy by the name of Mr. Herbert, I was soon busy. He used to run a splendid shop which was a pawnbroker's and model shop and he would bring me all the materials I needed to build model ships and aeroplanes. That was in the days when the things had to be carved from solid wood, not just gluing together pieces of plastic. A little balsa wood carved up can make an awful lot of shavings and when the beds were wheeled out for the daily sweep-up my place in the ward was shown by a great semi-circle of wood shavings and sawdust. Still, no one ever complained. I even graduated to flying models. It was quite a large ward and there was ample room for model gliders. I was there for just over two weeks and was discharged with instructions on how to give myself injections of insulin twice a day for the rest of my life. It didn't particularly bother me – I just didn't give it much thought! Looking back over thirty years and nearly 20,000 jabs later I have nothing to complain about. In fact, I am sure I would not have enjoyed such good health had I not been diabetic, as to keep fit one has to take an intelligent interest in a balanced and regular diet which is not what the average "healthy" person does. My one regret is that this barred me from National Service. I would have been very pleased to have gone into the R.A.F. – I think my life would have been very different. Not necessarily better, but certainly different.

After discharge from hospital I still had to return to the clinic at Bury St. Edmunds once a week for a check-up and this got to fortnightly and then monthly. It meant many days off school which suited me fine. I used to return home for lunch and sometimes I would have an insulin reaction which would not wear off until about 2 o'clock, but that was far too late to return to school! It dawned on me before long that as a roll call was not taken in the afternoon I was not missed! Perhaps this diabetic game had its uses after all. Thus many a time I would slide into the shed for the afternoon and avoid a lot of homework, compulsory games and other noxious activities. There was the question of the school certificate examination coming up of course, but that did not cause me any loss of sleep. My little scheme remained undetected until a few days before I was to leave school in the June when our games master casually asked me where I had been the previous afternoon when the timetable laid down that I was due to cavort with the other miserable souls on the field. I was unable to provide a suitable excuse to satisfy this mean man and with delight he made it clear that the matter would be brought to the notice of the headmaster without delay. Anyway the headmaster obviously had more sense than old "grumble guts" and nothing was said, and in a few days I departed for good from those hallowed halls without the all important certificate.

I really had no idea what I should do for a career, but Father insisted I join him at the works at Wymondham, which I did without enthusiasm. So we duly moved to "The Limes" and with regret left our little home at 49 Croxton Road and all my Thetfordian friends.

"The Limes" was a big block of four cold, damp, five-bedroomed houses, which were fine in the days of servants and big fires in each room, but Mum and I were like two peas in an otherwise empty pod. I used to sleep on the top floor and the next room became my workshop. The town was about a mile away and I had to bike two miles to the Works, which was annoying as I could see the place from the bedroom window.

From the start I never did really fit into the furniture works – that is, while Father was alive – and by the time he departed to his Maker it was too late. Anyway, in August I started and because of my diet and injections I went from nine to half-past four which even today is not an arduous spell of labour, but some of my days seemed very long and dreary. Occasionally an interesting job would come along, like a major breakdown of the main engine and then I would work with the relish and enthusiasm I learned to enjoy when challenged in later life. I don't mind how late I work if the job is interesting, but if the job is boring I'm like the modern automatons in factories – I get frustrated. I can understand them getting bolshy.

I became the odd-job lad, in that jobs which no one else wanted like making new wheelbarrows, building repairs, concreting, and eventually sharpening cutters for the planing machines, saws and the endless things that wear out in a sawmill and machine shop would fall to my lot. The job which I disliked most, and unfortunately was good at, was grinding and setting the cutters for the automatic lathe. This was a machine that would take a square table leg and turn it into a fancy profile in two minutes. The leg was slowly rotated and fed into a set of high speed cutters, each blade ground and set for a particular small part of the profile. The cutters had to be reground and sharpened with an oil stone until they were the original shape. I never did manage to hand that job on to anyone else.

After about a year I began to think about motorising my transport, and at that time several engines were on the market that could be fitted to an ordinary push bike. Most of them were about 25 cc and drove by means of a friction wheel on the tyre, which did a great deal of "no good" to the tread. There were various schemes to make the things grip in the wet. Some makers adopted a roller resembling a small concrete wheel, others ribbed aluminium or anything seemingly more suited to rip the tyre to bits rather than drive the bike. One of the better machines was called the Cyclemaster, which was a complete replacement rear wheel which was fitted with a 25 cc two-stroke with clutch all in an enlarged hub. I came across one of these machines fitted to a bike and I rode it home after parting with about 40 quid. Looking back I was rather diddled by the shop as the manager had been using the thing to travel to and from the shop! So I paid new money for a second-hand bike. However, that machine gave me great enjoyment, not only taking me to the works but much farther afield. I never did wear that little engine up in spite of it buzzing away at millions of revs. Eventually I passed it on in exchange for money.

Our timber had always been moved around the yard and into the sawmill by a 5-ton crane built in 1902. It ran up and down 200 yards of 7-foot gauge track and was built by Stothart and Pitt. As this machine was reaching retiring age – in fact, had probably passed it by several score – Father decided that he would have a new one. Not any old crane off the shelf, but a bespoke crane built by Taylor and Hubbard. This was to cost over £4,000; a lot of money when old Granny Crane would have groaned and wheezed her way onwards and upwards with a little overhaul. Unlike the new monster she had exposed connecting rods and disc cranks, so not only did she work well but, like British justice, she could be seen to work! The new crane had all her interesting parts – cranks, eccentrics – shut up in an iron box. How anyone could expect a steam engine to run properly with all her essentials shut up in a lot of messy oil I shall never understand. She must have been designed by a lot of new-fangled people who didn't understand these things – probably never even got their nails dirty.

The day came when the low loader arrived and rails were laid to run the new crane on to our track and poor old Granny Crane was shoved up the other end of the track where she quietly died under the scrap-man's hammer. One of my saddest memories.

Built in 1952, the Taylor and Hubbard must have been one of the last steam cranes made. It served us well for about twelve years when the boiler was condemned due to using hard water from our deep borehole which caused pitting of the fire-box crown. Old Billy, who used to drive the Stothart and Pitt, did not take too well to the new crane so eventually I became the official driver. I became quite proficient at driving and could slip the dog teeth of the various controls with ease. I remember unloading a drug of small sycamore once and having the lorry away and the timber stacked up in twenty minutes. I used to spin those wheels like Casey Jones!Eventually I was faced with the dilemma of a useless boiler and not able to afford the £600 for a new one, so we very reluctantly decided to convert the crane to diesel. We found a Meadows engine in a scrap yard and I coupled this with a gear box from a diesel shunting locomotive and we were again in the lifting business. The conversion was a great success and worked well, but the ease and flexibility of operation of the steam engine was gone. Nevertheless we got out of a £600 muddle for one hundred quid!

Father used to take me on his timber-buying expeditions. One of our suppliers would ring and say he had some timber that would suit us. It would be measured up and a price agreed for delivery into the yard. After measuring the length and circumference the cubic content was calculated and a bark allowance made depending on the type of wood. For example, elm had a big allowance as the bark can be two to three inches thick, but ash or sycamore perhaps less than half an inch. To illustrate my ineptitude with figures, in my early days Father set me to working out the cost of a drug load of timber at, I think, about five bob (25 pence) a cubic Foot. After sweating in the office all afternoon I came up with the value of £17, which pleased him no end! I can still see the look of disgust and rage at his near imbecile son who was only £287 out!

Most of the hardwoods would be left stacked in the yard for at least a year, then they would be cross cut with an incredible machine which was a reciprocating blade driven by a small engine mounted on two wood bearers with wheels on one end and the other end fixed to the log to be sawn. This thing would chug away and be through an average log in about 15 minutes. Eventually the same job was done with a chain saw in as many seconds. After cutting to length, which could be up to 20 feet, the log was drawn into the sawmill by a steam winch which got its steam from the stationary boiler which burned all our waste material and provided heat for the kilns where the timber was dried. The log saw would reduce the timber to boards or planks which were then carted away to the seasoning yard where they were stacked "splined" so that air could circulate around each board for another nine months. They would then be carted, again by hand, to another part of the sawmill for selective cutting and taken to one of the two kilns for a fortnight's wet heat. So, from the time the timber was felled to the time it left as furniture, was around three years. All this man-handling and carting was O.K. in the days of low wages, but to me it was a dreadful waste of time. With this in mind I acquired an old tractor unit from a British Railways articulated lorry and made it into a flat truck. We took everything off that vehicle that was not strictly necessary. This included the radiator and all forms of engine cooling. She only had to run for ten minutes at a time and used to groan round the yard, but never did protest at over-heating unlike the poor chaps who did it by hand before she arrived!

Early in the 1950s a plot of land came on the market near the works and it was decided to build a house there and move from "The Limes" and in due course Mother and I moved into "Larkhill". My feet were sufficient to get me to the mill as the journey was only about 300 yards, but in that distance I had to cross a private road which proved to be the spur to a great many experiments in communications.

I set my mind to finding a way of linking Railway Works and "Larkhill" – any thoughts of employing a conventional telephone were not entertained for one moment! The crux of the matter was crossing the road. All sorts of ideas came to mind, amongst which was a system of earth electrodes, one pair on either side of the road so that the current passed between them under the road. A number of experiments were carried out to see what happened and a surprising thing came to light. If a pair of earth electrodes were placed even quite close together and a suitable electrical signal applied then the signal could be detected quite a long way off. Obviously an electrical disturbance was being radiated further afield as well. This was most interesting and opened up all sorts of possibilities. But how to find out? The garden was madly excavated and great sheets of galvanized steel, etc., were buried. Amplifiers were built for transmitting and receiving and a horizontal coil of wire about two feet square built into the car. The car was then driven round the plot in ever increasing circles to find the field strength. Just as I was going to bed one night I suddenly wondered if this effect would work in water. We had a static tank at the works which was built for fire-fighting during the war, so it was a simple matter to try the idea out. The tank was about 30 feet square, two aluminium plates were connected to the side and these to an amplifier. A pair of head-phones connected to two probes soon established that the signal was well and truly radiated throughout the tank. One very interesting point soon arose, and that was the very marked directional effect of the receiving probes. No matter where they were inserted in the water, a position could be found in their relationship with one another where the signal faded completely to nil. I had noticed a similar effect in ground transmissions, but this was much more pronounced in water. This opened several possibilities and I jumped at the idea of using this effect for navigation of ships.

I had an ex-R.A.F. inflatable dinghy at the time, so this was duly provided with a receiving electrode on each side and the car loaded up with the transmitting amplifier. We stopped at Thetford to pick up a like-minded friend and off we went to the river. A transmitting plate was put into the water at each side and about a couple of hundred yards away I launched myself in the dinghy wearing a pair of head-phones and blindfolded! I was soon able to turn the dinghy so as to receive no signal and found at this point I was directed downstream to the transmitter. Thus, blindfold and paddling to keep the receiver signal at zero, I navigated directly to the transmitting plates. Very interesting.

At this point I thought there might be some money in the game, so I duly drew up a provisional patent and at the same time wrote to the Admiralty with a description of my findings. The reply was full of the same wild enthusiasm that the government displayed for aeroplanes in 1910. So I wrote to the Army and had a most charming letter of thanks which mentioned that a similar method of communication was employed to a very limited extent in the First War – very interesting, but not bringing forth vast funds of money in recognition of inventiveness and unstinting devotion to the furtherance of scientific knowledge ! Any port in a storm so, thrashing the typewriter ribbon to shreds writing a witty and enthralling account of the experiments, I sent the details off to a popular scientific magazine which resulted in a similar reply to that received from the armed forces.

Nothing daunted, further experiments were carried out, this time in the remote control of model boats. A little twin-screw model was built about 18 inches long and fitted with a couple of plates underneath feeding a hearing aid amplifier and a set of tuned reeds. These reeds were adjusted so that when a certain note was received one reed would vibrate in sympathy and operate that control. Thus, by sending suitable notes the boat could be steered or go full ahead or astern. And the jolly little boat worked! The only snag was the directional effect, which meant that I needed two sets of transmitting plates so when the model was in a null position for the set in use the other set could be switched in and control restored. The transmitter was very simple, just a set of buzzers with no amplifiers or other gadgetry. All very splendid. I felt sure I'd be able to sell the idea for early in the model control experiments I contacted a firm that specialised in radio control gear and they seemed most interested and gave me every encouragement. Thus fooled by my own enthusiasm I prepared demonstration models and set forth in search of riches to the other side of the country. Upon arriving at the firm, I may say by appointment, I was met by complete apathy and disinterest. To be fair someone did just come and look in the boot of the car, but I might have just as well displayed a bowl of cold sprouts.

Anyway it had been a nice journey and I had stayed with some agreeable friends, so all was not lost. You live and learn.

Just for the record, I never did use the system to communicate with the works. I found I could hire a wire from the G.P.O. and provide my own telephone to be connected at either end. The total cost, just £4 per year.

It must have been just after the Suez fuel crisis that I got to thinking about building an electric bike. One thing which set this off was the existence of a large 12-volt electric motor lying in the workshop of a friend. This I bought for a few shillings and a chassis was planned out. The frame was to be of wood, there being a lot about, and after all ships and aeroplanes were built of wood so why not a motorbike? The backbone was a couple of ash bearers about 3½ inches by 1¼ inches set on edge about 3 inches apart. The rear wheels were between these at the extreme back and at the front a roughly triangular plywood box rose up to support the front forks. These were provided with roller bearings. The forks were bent and shaped from steel plate and welded to a spindle with conventional handle bars at the top. I had a couple of the old small, heavy trade bike front wheels, the rear one fitted with a large chain sprocket. Drive was originally through a two-speed gearbox which was later discarded as of no advantage. Transversely under the seat was a battery box holding lead acid batteries giving 18 volts at 75 amp hours. The result was more of a scooter than a bike, but the appearance I found quite acceptable. In common with all electric vehicles the performance was not startling, but the silence was quite uncanny, there was no pollution and old ladies couldn't hear you coming! I found the machine of most use around town, but after a couple of years the batteries gave out and I could not face the expense of replacement. One thing I am very proud of is that I passed my motor cycle driving test on this machine! I well remember my anxiety in expecting the batteries to give out before the examiner had finished with me!

Soon after completing the bike I got to thinking about something special on four wheels. I suppose the thing that acted as a catalyst this time was a 1931 Austin Seven rusting away in a garden a few miles away. After parting with ten one-pound notes she was towed home. You could do that in those

David King on the all electric wooden bike

days, the law was much more reasonable about towing things. The devil had not yet found how easy it was to implant meddlesome thoughts in the minds of idle politicians. A Saturday afternoon was all it took to get the body off the poor old Austin and we soon had her running in her nakedness around the mill yard.

During the next few weeks my usual optimism was running on in top gear convinced it was but a matter of days to overhaul the chassis and engine and build a body, in wood of course. Actually it took three months of spare time, and using some that really should not have been spare.

The chassis and engine were soon dismantled, the former engine was re-bored, a new inlet manifold made up in copper pipe and fitted with an SU carburettor. The chassis was de-rusted, re-bushed, straightened out and refurbished. Brakes – well, I don't think that is quite the term for those on the Austin 7: shall we say the gentle retarders? – were improved as far as possible. The biggest and easiest step in this direction was by replacing the stranded cable to the back drums with piano wire which, unlike the original, is very reluctant to stretch. Thus I could lock the back wheels, which did not seem to retard progress as much as it should. It just stopped the back wheels going round, which shows how much work is done by front brakes on any vehicle.

Attention was then turned to the bodywork. Like all my things it just "growed" from the bottom. It soon became evident that the whole project would benefit from making the complete front from the driver's seat easily removable, so that all one had to do was to remove the petrol connection, unplug the lights, and unscrew six wing nuts and she was naked again. As I proved more than once, the engine could be out of the car and on the workshop floor in one hour. Much time and trouble was spent running round the scrap yards for spares and replacements. A few things had to be bought new, like the radiator and head and tail lights. The petrol tank was a four gallon jerry can. I think the total cost was about £120 and I enjoyed every penny of it. The car was certainly fun to drive, as long as driver and passengers were fresh air fanatics. The little Austin has an "A" frame chassis, with the apex at the front, which means the side members pass on their way to the back springs under the backsides of the driver and passenger. This limits the minimum height of the seats. This matters not in the saloon, but in a low sporty car it means that one sits on the car rather than in it.

The little Austin gave us a lot of fun and never let us down, except for knocking the big ends out once, but we rattled our way home without them. Next day the engine was out and the rods re-metalled and machined in the lathe and back on the road in a jiffy. Try doing that with your Mini! Eventually the car went the way of all cars – we parted for money. I regretted the sale and soon bought it back, only to let it go again to a member of the family who ran foul of the recently introduced M.O.T. test. Undaunted, he set forth over the horizon and the Austin was not seen again. One thing I am sure of, she did not go for scrap. Firewood maybe, but not scrap – such a harsh word.

By an extraordinary chain of events I was drawn into the steam launch game. I was visiting our local scrap yard and the owner had just come home with his pick-up and on the back was a fascinating piece of rusty iron that looked as if it could be a steam launch engine. "Teark ut away an see wot yew can dew withut." I didn't need to be asked twice and the engine was soon in my workshop. It turned out to be a twin cylinder of about 3 inches bore and

The rebodied – rebuilt Austin 7. David at the wheel

stroke. The extraordinary thing was that the cast-iron names imprinted on the steam chests had been carefully filed away and, try as we might, the maker's name could not be deciphered, but it was thought to be a Butterly. Eventually the engine was back to new condition and put under the bench until a use could be found for it. I did not think it was likely that I would be able to install it in a hull worthy of such an engine, but somebody else might. Then a strange coincidence happened. A friend of mine sat opposite an elderly chap in a train reading the "Model Engineer". This turned out to be Frank Drewson, a ship's engineer, who had a passion for steam boats in general and kept his own at Brundall on the Norfolk Broads. The little marine engine was soon mentioned and addresses exchanged. Eventually the first of many long letters arrived on my door mat showing great interest in the Butterly and as Frank was at sea a friend of his would inspect and photograph the engine. Thus I made the acquaintance of Frank Denton, who soon became a valued friend. The Butterly was installed in the "Raloo" at Brundall. The "Raloo" had been a ship's lifeboat, seemingly a million years ago. The hull was so tender, or to be exact rotten, that all boatyards on the Broads had refused to pull her out of the water for fear of breaking the hull in half. She had a little cabin and Frank used to spend his leave on board. He was a remarkable chap whose whole passion in life was his steamer. His father had been a steam ship designer, and his grandfather burned to death on top of a boiler when he had gone up to free a sticking safety valve which lifted and blew the poor chap over where he remained undiscovered until the next day.

Frank used to make all his fittings, pipework and steam pumps on board his tramp steamer and bring them to Brundall for installation. Actually he had built "Raloo's" engine himself and after trials found it was not quite powerful enough, so built another smaller one and bolted this on the end of the original. This little helper engine became mine when the Butterly was installed, so I was now on the way to being a steamboat owner. I only needed a boat and a boiler. Some years previously I sold a stationary engine and vertical boiler and I remembered the buyer saying at the time that he was mainly interested in the engine, so I got in touch with him and the boiler came home. I now had a perfect engine and boiler for a steamer. I started to look out for a hull, and sure enough someone advertised a partly completed sailing dinghy at Thorpe. She was 11 feet long and ideal for me. I think I paid about £25 and brought her home on the car roof. It was not long before engine, boiler and hull were brought together and we were all set for a launching in October, 1958.

About that time I met a girl. Some friends had introduced us and I found her most attractive, if time consuming. The week after we met the little steamer was ready for launching and what better arrangement than to combine the two interests and invite my new friend on the maiden voyage. To my amazement she accepted. On reflection the risks were great for there we were in a boat that had never been afloat, with an engine that had never driven her propeller, a second-hand boiler, and me not necessarily in control! But everything went splendidly, except we were daft enough to go nearly to Norwich and arrived back at the moorings at dusk with the aid of the paddle having run out of coal. Valerie said she actually enjoyed it! Shortly after that we went to see the film "The African Queen" and decided to name our little steamer after the heroine, Rosie Allnutt. Unlike everyone else we usually seemed to go steaming in the winter and many times we have been down the cut from our moorings crunching through the ice. Not the best idea in a ply hull as they are likely to get cut through at the water line! So we just used to rock the boat so the ice did not make all the holes in one place. Eventually "Rosie" was sold and went to live on the Thames and twelve years and many buckets of coal later I found her still giving good service, except someone had pinched her whistle.

I had enough sense to realise that anyone so outstandingly intelligent as to enjoy my eccentric interests was not to be treated lightly and I thought I would try to put my relationship with Valerie on a more permanent footing. Not only that but I was spending far too long on the telephone in the evenings when I should be making things and to my amazement she had similar ideas. It's unusual to find anyone who likes steam, coal, oil, grease, tools, wheels and all the other things that go with an engineering "nut", so if you are lucky enough to find one best stick to 'em. We were married in July 1959.

The furniture trade was not doing so well, but Father was still very much in command in spite of his years. I did not realise how things were going, otherwise I might have used up some of my reserves of optimism. I began to look at other products to use our skill with timber and had an idea for a folding caravan. After much sketching our Foldavan was born and I must say I am still rather proud of the design. It was built of an ash frame and mahogany ply and all polished inside. The folding could be done in under two minutes

Rosie Allnutt with Valerie aboard, 1959

by one person. In fact we had one customer who could have his kettle on the gas in 60 seconds! They were very neat. Not only did the height come down to 4 feet 6 inches, the width was also reduced to the same measurement from 6 feet 6 inches when open. We sold these for £218 and actually made about twenty. Some are still in use today, nearly twenty years later. The first one we sold has just passed from father to son.

One day someone drew my attention to an advert for ex-army pontoons for sale. This made me think and visions of a paddle steamer materialised. After all, by now Valerie had produced Sally and Richard and how could anyone be so unthinking as to bring up two children without such a basic item of family life. A friend and I took a trip one Sunday to Peterborough and picked out the best pontoon we could find and handed over the princely sum of £25. After a week or so a lorry arrived in the yard just as Father was leaving for lunch. I have never seen him so furious! We soon had the load off and put as far out of sight as possible.

Shortly after this, one Tuesday morning I was met with the news that Father was unwell and would remain in the house that day. This was the first time he had not opened up the office at 8.00 a.m. and the first time I had ever known him to be in anything but perfect health. Within a day or so he was admitted to a nursing home in Norwich and died a few weeks later, purely of old age, at 79.

The furniture trade was very slow and we decided to concentrate more on the office furniture side. We had one very good customer and we bent over backwards to oblige him. However, I could see the danger in this as our goodwill with the company virtually rested with one man and if he should be displaced that market could well vanish overnight.

I found an old Morris two-ton van, the sort made of hardboard, looking like a tea chest with a wheel at each corner. I painted it up and lettered it with my newly thought up trademark and she looked very smart. We could now give a jolly good service, instead of having to rely on the railway, who were better at losing our furniture than delivering it. They lost a whole truck-load once – six weeks later it was found in a siding in Cumberland. Amusing in retrospect, but not funny when we were short of customers. Our van was a godsend. More than once an order received on the telephone would be delivered within two hours. The mechanics of the van were not as good as the bodywork. After all, only woodworm could destroy that and they were old friends of ours in the timber trade.

While on the subject of transport I must relate the saga of King and his Rolls (not The, just me). Valerie and I became intrigued with advertisements at the time in the motor sporting Press of what we now call Classic cars. It seemed that for the price of half a new Ford we could have a Rolls-Royce or Bentley or some other piece of exotica. We wrote around to one or two dealers and received the usual rose-tinted descriptions. Eventually we settled with a dealer in the Midlands who would consider swapping the Jowett Javelin we had than in part exchange for a Rolls. So we packed our toothbrushes one weekend in the Autumn and set forth to Staffordshire in the fog. I must explain that I had been using some cheap oil in the car engine. We bought this by the 50-gallon drum for use in the works and Father had full confidence in it as this was an all purpose lubricant for anything from a grandfather clock to a 75 horsepower diesel. We were about half way when I found the oil pressure dropping alarmingly and we had to find a garage every 20 miles and fill up with thicker and thicker oil. We arrived at about 3 o'clock with the engine feeling rather sick to say the least. The dealer had kindly offered to put us up and we had arrived at the most charming spot you would wish to find in the English countryside. It was in a valley, a newish house set in the hillside and the only sounds were birds and a rippling stream. Mr. Dealer soon introduced himself and his charming wife and the manservant. He had a quick look at the Javelin and I did mention that I thought the crankshaft bearings might be a little slack, but to my amazement this was dismissed as a mere trifle that his mechanic could correct in a trice . . . and what a nice car the Javelin was and how clever I had been to paint it so nicely. We went in to have a meal and luckily Mr. Manservant took kindly to us, as we had been warned that if he didn't we would be unlikely to get fed during our stay. We spent a delightful evening talking cars and eventually made our way to bed. We soon found that the only spare bed was a single, but we would have been glad of a bale of straw that night. It is difficult to put into words our impression of the house. It appeared that as funds became available certain work would be carried out until the money was exhausted. This would explain the half papered toilet with a gold plated candelabra hanging from the ceiling over the seat! Before we found our room and upon opening an upstairs door we were confronted with another Bentley! How do you get a Bentley into an upstairs bedroom you may ask. Well the house was built into the side of the hill, so what would have been upstairs inside was the garage outside!

The next morning, after enjoying Mr. Manservant's breakfast, we were promised that Mr. Mechanic would arrive with dear old Blue Angel – a Rolls. I really must try and convey our host's attitude to cars. This was quite unique and unlike the usual dealer. The whole value of a car in his eyes had no connection in any remote way to the age or condition either bodily or mechanically – and I must stress this was long before the days of the M.O.T. test. The value of any vehicle in Mr. Dealer's eyes lay purely in the character of the car. The tyres might be bald, the wood-framing might be disintegrating with dry rot or woodworm, the brakes were of little importance so long as they would stop the car eventually, and the engine was only to move the car – preferably forwards – in some acceptable way. The true value lay in the aura, the charisma or the charm – indeed the beauty in the eye of the beholder.

Later in the morning Mr. Dealer decided that the car for us was the 1933 Rolls 20/24 which he called "The Fisherman's" because it had been re-bodied for a keen angler. After inspecting the car we were pleased to say it was one of the least tatty, but there was some reason why it was not immediately available so we could not drive it home. This put us in a pickle to say the least as I knew jolly well that the Javelin would not get us home. There was, however, another Rolls which took my eye and seemed reasonably road-worthy. Thus we offered to take this one – A Mulliner – home leaving the Javelin plus £90. The understanding was that I would work on the car and exchange it for "The Fisherman's" when she was ready – promised in a week or two. So we set off for Norfolk late in the afternoon, only to find at dusk that the rear lights did not work. However, we managed to put that right and eventually arrived home very late and wondering what sort of a nut I was to have exchanged my Javelin for such a heap of junk. As the weeks went by I gradually tidied up the car. I set to work to re-trim everything in front of the driver as I reckoned that this would be most likely to impress a purchaser! After many 'phone calls to the Midlands and receiving many ingenious excuses every time as to why "The Fisherman's" was not ready, we were getting a little angry. It was now into the Spring and at one time the snow over the hill was said to prevent any vehicular access. The old Mulliner was whining her sweet way about with more and more uncertainty, the tyres were threatening to show canvas and I had had some hair-raising experiences with the brakes. This was caused by passing through a heavy shower and water getting into the power servo which assisted the brakes from the gearbox. The effect was that as soon as the driver touched the brake all hell would be let loose as the servo grabbed on the anchors for all it was worth. The whole front of the car would leap about until I was afraid it would break in half! I eventually got an idea of where the trouble was and left an electric fire on the offending servo all night and thereafter all was well.

Eventually we heard that "The Fisherman's" was still not ready but there was another that might do us and we said "yes please" with both hands. So we agreed that the car would be brought to Cambridge with another that was to be delivered. So, off to Cambridge to meet Mr. Dealer who arrived with his wife and only ONE car . . . and that was not ours! What a pity they could not bring ours, but at the last minute it was found that the brakes were not up to the high standard required by Mr. Dealer before he could possibly consider parting with the car to such valuable customers. Never mind, would we come and have lunch, and the new customer accepted his Rolls with joy and we went off to an hotel where the new customer treated us all! After fond farewells to their customer Mr. Dealer and his wife told us how sorry they were that we had come for nothing and would we be so kind as to take them to Bedford so they could catch the train home! Such is the charm of the man. This we did and the poor old Mulliner limped her way eventually back to Wymondham. Whatever else can be said that car was quiet. She just used to glide about without a sound. All pieces of machinery have their "natural" speeds and hers was about 43 miles per hour. Forty-one was too slow and 44 too fast, but 43 – lovely.

After what seemed a million years "The Fisherman's" arrived at Wymondham and we enjoyed her for a year or two. It was nice to have had the experience, but I cannot say I have any inclination to have another Rolls of the Thirties. Much older perhaps, but to my mind Rolls-Royce cars steadily became less interesting as the years went by after about 1929.

One day I spotted an Alvis for sale at £250 in a local dealers and we fell in love with it straight away – and what a bargain. It was a 3-litre TA 21 and a superb car in every way. I sold the Rolls back to Mr. Dealer and I think she went to the States like so many others.

I soon found that the Alvis was suffering from low oil pressure, so I stripped the engine down and found the oil pump worn out. The engine was rebuilt and I repainted the body by hand to the correct original colour scheme and she was a really beautiful car. I cannot decide whether the Javelin or the Alvis was the best car that I have ever had.

The paddle steamer was progressing nicely, as usual there being far more work than I ever visualised. She was fitted out with a self-contained engine room aft and a cabin with gas hotplate, sink, double bunk and a forward steering position in the cabin from which the engine could be controlled. The boiler was a vertical for which I had made an oil burner, and a launch engine in one corner of the engine room driving the stern paddle wheel through chains and a counter shaft. The engine, an Uncle Tom Cobley sort of affair, drove a wondrous set of pumps through this shaft for doing such things as maintaining the vacuum, filling the boiler, emptying the bilges, pressurising the fuel tank and all. The whole plant got very complex and I remember there were fifteen hand valves to control the flow of water, steam and fuel.

Upon completion the whole vessel was transported on to our static water tank at the back of the works to try running the engine under load and to see if the whole damn thing would float or sink. This last eventuality was not beyond speculation among the workmen! Anyway she was a pretty sight and did indeed float. "Charlie Allnutt", as she had to be called after our adventure with "Rosie", was ultimately carried by lorry to Norwich and launched into the River Yare. She gave us no end of pleasure and no trouble at all.

The furniture trade continued to decline and our business with it, and it soon became obvious that we could not carry on much longer in spite of bringing out new designs. The office furniture side was just holding its own, the caravans were selling in ones and twos, but we needed three years' stock of timber to allow for seasoning and drying and our normal stock had been allowed to get rather low towards the end of Father's time. This, added to rising costs, overheads and rates, all pointed to one thing – we either had to borrow heavily and reorganize or we had to rethink the whole business that Father gave birth to and that seemed to die with him. I talked it over with my brother and we decided to close down. As has happened before in my life Lady Luck or Divine Providence was with us. Our industrial neighbours called one day – perhaps it was just coincidence – and asked if we would consider selling them the sawmill site. We would and did. The next problem was to keep going and run down at the same time. It was sad to think that our employees would have to go; one in particular had come to Father for work and was promised employment for a fortnight – and here he was still with us thirty-five years later. I had known many since I was a nipper. They were more friends than employees. Some found work, but sadly others never did. Our machine shop foreman met up with a chap with capital and they took over some of the machinery and carried on with the office furniture for several years, but that too gradually folded.

Having reached the bottom of the pit the only way was up, so the ending of the Railway Works gave me new impetus for the future. I had not liked the way things were developing in the business world and came to the conclusion that a quiet life, doing what has become known as one's "thing", has a lot to recommend it. Accordingly I set about drawing my horns in and reducing expenditure all I could. An auction was arranged for the machinery and stock. This took place in October 1963 and brought in some useful cash. In the meantime we had been house-hunting – obviously we were looking for somewhere with a potential workshop. We had parted with the beloved Alvis and now had a Mini Traveller, which was a big asset, a faithful work horse and cheaper to run.

While this was going on my sister had arrived from Australia as Mother had become very ill with cancer, so this threw another cloud over all of us. Eventually Mother went into a nursing home.

Just before my sister, Barbara, returned to Australia we visited a place for

The Foldavan with Valerie and Sally, 1961

sale in North Norfolk and quite liked what we saw. I particularly liked the 60 feet by 25 feet shed but Valerie was not too keen on the bungalow so we did not jump at the idea. Then the agent rang and suggested we make a bid as "Greenways", as it was called, had been on the market for some time. So I named a very low figure with tongue in cheek and the agent said perhaps not quite that low, suggested an amount which I could afford and in the end a bargain was struck. We now had a three-bedroom bungalow with brick office and garage and the workshop, set in three-quarters of an acre of land overlooking a gentle Norfolk valley. All very quiet and really exactly what we needed if only we had realised before that this was what we wanted – not only the place but to get out of the "rat race".

Our old Morris cardboard van now had to work in earnest. Thirty-two journeys loaded with all the machinery and materials I might find useful from Railway Works to "Greenways". The back axle did not quite disgorge its entrails but the old engine was drinking oil. I cadged old sump oil and we used to fill up every journey. When, years later, I dismantled the engine it was so full of carbon that the internal workings had just carved room for themselves to rotate!

Just as we moved into "Greenways" Mother died quietly. It was sad to think that she was not to see our new home as she was always concerned about our future. No one could have wished for a better Mother. I'm sure she knows now that "Greenways" was the spot for us.

After my lifelong pleasant association with all things driven by steam and the fact that people seemed to want engines that I had built, I decided that I would try and earn my living just building or rebuilding engines. The first thing to do was to set up the workshop. This took the best part of a year. Naturally all my equipment was the old 110 volts d.c. so I decided to invest in a new diesel generator instead of going on the mains. After many inquiries I found that the engine we had been using for standby lighting could not be bettered, so I bought a new one for £145 and coupled this to a generator. That engine has been a gem. It has had thousands of gallons of fuel through it and fourteen years later has only been decarbonised and the valves ground in once. Naturally they are not made any more! They were too good; no built-in obsolescence. What future is there for a firm building engines like that?

At the end of the first year everything was pretty well set up and I thought to myself "Righto world. Here I am. Come and beat a path to my door". But the world did not hear – well, not straightaway. So I had to build something on spec. I found an old motor bike, actually a 1921 Sparkbrook, which I bought for a few pounds and brought home in the back of the Mini! I set to work and restored it to new condition and was amazed to sell it for enough to make having done it very worthwhile. Years later I found that there are only five left in existence! If only I had hung on to it. Still, one must avoid greed at all costs and can only do what appears right at the time.

There was still no work coming in, so I tried a few adverts in a specialist magazine. Out of the blue came a letter one day from a chap in North Wales. He had a 25-foot hull and a boiler and would I like to build him an engine. At last! I could see this order as a springboard so I quoted him a ridiculously low price of £200, a quarter to be paid with the order, another quarter when the patterns were made and the castings arrived from the foundry, and a further quarter when the engine ran and the rest upon delivery. Back came a cheque for £50 and we were away!

Apart from having to make two crankshafts all went well and I experienced the first of many thrills when one of my engines ran for the first time. The engine was delivered to North Wales, but soon after the owner decided to give up the project as an opportunity arose for him to purchase some property. The engine went to a collector much nearer Norfolk and has remained in his museum ever since and has not run since it left here. Seems a pity not to give it a run now and again. Whilst working on the engine the thought came to me that it would be fun and useful to have a traction engine. The supply of steam would be of immense value for testing other engines. I tracked down several engines that might be for sale with the help of friends and had one or two near purchases. The trouble is that owners get so attached to their engines that when it actually comes to parting their minds change. I remember going into Suffolk where I had been offered an engine and we were invited to go over and see it steamed up. At the end of the afternoon the owner had clearly had a change of heart and nothing would induce him to sell. On another occasion I drove over to Staffordshire to see a Burrell general-purpose engine. At the time I had never driven or steered an engine on the road and as soon as we arrived I got straight out of the car on to the foot-plate, whereupon the driver, who had been in the game all his life, opened the regulator and we shot off on to a housing estate with me steering. Anyone who knows Burrells will realise what a hairy experience that was, as the steering is very low geared and the wheel has to be spun like mad to steer the front axle. And this with children and lamp posts seemingly coming within inches of the wheels. I don't know how, but we managed to get back to the yard without mishap and in the end decided that this particular engine was not for me. Eventually a friend suggested I should have a word with the owner of an extremely pretty 6-horsepower McLaren. My reaction was that I was quite sure that this could not possibly be for sale. Nevertheless I followed it up and eventually she came home. Not, I may say, without the now familiar "yes, I will sell" and "no, I'd rather sell my grandmother".

This engine was built for the military and the tale was that she was one of a batch of twenty-seven, most of which went to France in the First War. She was built in 1918 but stayed this side of the Channel by the skin of her teeth for she was taken into use at Chatham Docks. No more was known of the history until 1940 when she worked for agricultural contractors in Lincolnshire and was later sold to a contractor in Essex, where tree hauling and such like was carried out. Like most engines at that time just after the war she was sold for scrap for just £8. Standing on a disused aerodrome for about a year she was spotted by an enthusiast who had a critical eye for a handsome piece of machinery and bought her from the scrap dealer for £11. Then she started on a long trail of restoration and was soon seen at engine rallies in Suffolk and Norfolk.

Upon the death of the owner the McLaren was bequeathed to a close friend in South Norfolk who continued with the restoration work and painted the engine to a very high standard. The first time she was seen out was at the famous Raynham Day Rally in 1963 and a few years later she came to live here. We christened her "Dougal", for no better reason than that the name fitted.

A friend had cherished a lifelong ambition to own his own railway and in the end the only way he could see of becoming an Iron Road Proprietor was to build one himself. He started work on a simple engine, "Duncan", and laid a track round his garden. The locomotive progressed as far as the chassis and then a short cut was taken to get the train running by fitting a lawn mower engine to the poor thing! But it worked and they had a lot of fun. I became involved to finish the engine off. After all we could soon pop a new boiler into a suitable steam looking casing and the whole lot surrounded by pannier tanks. She was a great success in the garden and I remember a Breakfast Special run by the family, whereby at some early hour they were all to be found riding on the train eating cornflakes.

It was soon decided to show the train to the public and a trailer was equipped with portable track and earned a favourable reputation with local events. Soon demand was coming from far afield and the long suffering car had to be replaced with a Land-Rover to deal with the extra journeys.

Charlie Allnutt, 1963

"Duncan" had done very well but it became obvious that there was a much greater market amongst the public for a larger train so that adults could ride in greater comfort. It was decided that I should build a much larger locomotive for 10¼-inch gauge, but that is a story for later.

As a result of restoring an engine for one of the Thames steam launches – the "Woodland Lily" – a craft as elegant as her name, the owner approached me to build up a set of machinery for a long-term job he was tackling, this time a 50-foot Victorian launch to be called the "Esperanza". She had quite a history, having belonged to a firm of battery manufacturers and had therefore been electrically driven. Who else could afford to supply all those batteries? There must have been at least a ton of lead in them.

By some remarkable detective work the owner had located a beautiful twin cylinder engine built by Pope of Slough, which having been in a teaching establishment had never been run but merely dismantled by the students. This really was one of the most elegant and soundly designed engines I have ever come across. The slide bars had vee'd faces and all the valve gear pins had a very fine taper and they were as tight as new. It was necessary to make the boiler oil fired and I decided to build a burner like the one that was so successful in "Charlie Allnutt". That led me a right dance, as it seems that purely by chance I had got the first burner exactly right – you might say off the drawing board, or rather off the back of an envelope. My one complaint with newspapers is that they never leave me enough space in the margins to draw things. I find it so much easier to think if I have a pencil and paper. After thinking for half an hour often I find I may have only drawn one line, or even nothing at all. The thing is if I don't have a pencil as ideas flow I am inhibited by thinking I should be drawing as I might forget, but if I have the tools handy there is often no need to! Anyway after some experiments the burner seemed O.K. and it certainly heated the boiler and made steam.

In due course the plant was complete and my customer brought a trailer and Land-Rover and took the lot back to Surrey. I remember it was a bit of a rush at the last minute and I worked until 2.00 a.m., but it all went away on time. It was important as there was forthcoming a steamboat rally on the Thames and "Esperanza" was to be the flagship. A couple of days later I got a right earful on the 'phone. Somebody was really upset about something and would I go down and make this heap of junk work. Which I did, and it did, and everything went very well for the rally and a really elegant vessel "Esperanza" turned out to be. Would you believe there also was "Rosie Allnutt" chuffing along amongst all the vintage finery, holding her end up commendably. I felt very proud.

One Saturday morning we were sitting in the garden enjoying our ritual 10.30 coffee and the 'phone rang. A year previously I had sold "Charlie Allnutt" and she was on the Birmingham and Worcester canal and that was her new owner on the 'phone to say she had been completely burned out and was just a sodden mass of charcoal. What a sad bit of news. Luckily no one was hurt. Anyway it was an ill wind as her owner was so upset that work must be put in hand to build another. My reaction was "How splendid. I must build a real stern wheel engine just like those steam boats on the Mississippi". Everyone was thrilled with the idea and would I go over for a couple of days and talk it over, to which I readily agreed. I was soon off to Birmingham in my Spitfire (car, that is) and had a very fruitful discussion with the skipper and the famous Uffa Fox, who turned out to be a friend of the family and a great fan of "Charlie Allnutt". I returned to Norfolk with a head full of ideas and instructions to produce some bare general drawings as a guide to the construction of the hull which would have to accommodate the enormous engine. I had never produced any drawings that anyone else could be expected to understand, so I thought I had better build a proper drawing board. This I did and it probably set the whole project back a month! Eventually work was started on the hull and I began the engines here. I think that turned out to be one of the best pieces of work I have built at Suffield.

I must describe the Mississippi engine for the uninitiated. The idea is simplicity itself – the crankshaft is the actual paddle shaft across the stern of the boat. On either side of the hull is a cylinder which couples with the paddle shaft by the pitmans of connecting rods – as simple as a railway train! The boilers are usually forward; several on the bigger vessels are arranged across the boiler deck. On our small version the cylinders were 18 inch stroke by 3 inch bore. The pitmans were over 7 feet long and looked very handsome in polished ash. The paddle wheel was about 5 feet long and 5 feet diameter with eight blades of wood. The wheel frame was galvanised after all the welding was complete. One of the greatest thrills of my life was the first time I tested it on compressed air and saw the paddle shaft turn. I soon found it would run quite evenly at less than one revolution per minute. Imagine an engine running at the speed of a second hand on a clock – and in complete silence!

Eventually the hull was ready for the engines to be installed and I spent a very enjoyable few days fitting everything into the boat. Finally we had steam up and she ran well in the boat-shed. Back home again to await the completion of the upper works, which took several months. The great day for launching arrived. Back to the Midlands and amongst much television, radio and newspaper publicity the "Phoenix" was launched, steam was raised and the engines had to run in earnest.

It was a great relief when we turned on the steam and the wheel began to thrust impatiently at the water and the mooring ropes strained rhythmically with each dip of the paddle blades. The time came to cast off and with a blast of the original chime whistle from "Charlie Alnutt" we cast off and sailed down the canal. I must say how well everything went, especially considering that the engines had never run under load before.

Strangely enough, I had very few inquiries for paddle engines in spite of all the publicity, but that compound engine, built for Wales, brought letters from all over the world for years after a short magazine article. It was while building the paddle engine that I had a visit from a charming gentleman from Australia who, I remember, wore no socks, always drove in an open car and with whom I corresponded some years previously. It appeared that he had plans to build a steam pinnace near Sydney and would I be kind enough to restore the engine which he had out there.

This engine had quite a history. It was built in 1912 by Samuel White for the Admiralty and was installed in a naval steam pinnace. She found her way "Down Under" and was scrapped at the end of the last war and the engine given to a local school. In due course it was decided that tuition into the intricacies of the steam age was outdated and the White was put out for the scrapman. My client, who has a nose for such things, soon had it spirited away and in safe-keeping for twenty years, when the urge to build a pinnace came on. So the engine was crated carefully and after some weeks at sea arrived at Suffield, where it was stored away until the current work was finished.

Shortly after this new arrival a pick-up truck turned up with what must have been the most valuable piece of scrap I have ever seen. It was a Lifu boiler, built about 1900, composed entirely of copper and gunmetal. And this priceless article had laid in a field in Essex for years – the light-fingered deceived by the fact that it was in a rusty sheet metal case which hid from view the valuable copper. I decided to fit the boiler up with an oil burner and made up a head just as for the "Esperanza" boiler. It gave a flame the right size and shape, but had one sneaky fault which lurked in the design and defied me for

The £200 David King compound marine engine

weeks. It meant redrilling thousands upon thousands of holes until I found what I thought to be the right size and number. By now the burner head was starting to look like some piece of modern art. Eventually I felt that we had the job beaten and I was giving the burner a final run just to make sure. This time it had been going for one-and-a-half hours and the whole plant was running like a dream when – BANG – after weeks of work and goodness knows how many holes! So I threw the whole thing in the scrap and started to think again. I got hold of an old primus stove and tried to fathom out the reason for its shape and construction. I found that the burner head could run red hot and the cop could actually be lifted while running. But why did mine light back inside? Then the penny dropped. The flame was not getting back through the holes after all. The burner could run with the head red hot, therefore the essence was to get the vapour mixture into and out of the head as quickly as possible so that it would not have time to overheat and ignite. I set to and made a new head with this knowledge, with the internal spaces just big enough to pass that volume of gas. Result – perfection. The burner could be turned right down till the flame was just a faint blue haze and not so much as a gentle pop when it went out, and it would run all day. The boiler steamed like mad, working pressure in ten minutes and just a gentle hiss from the burner jet. End of panic!

This steam plant was very fully instrumented, showing the feed pump pressure, steam temperatures, boiler pressure, steam chest pressure, intermediate pressure and vacuum. And very handsome those instruments looked fitted to the top of the engine upon a polished mahogany panel with brass bound edges. Eventually I was completely satisfied and the whole unit was sprayed with a preservative, fitted with slings so it could be lifted by crane with no trouble and all crated up and shipped back "Down Under".

It was naturally with some relief that I learned from my new customer that the engine was installed after a few months and was giving every satisfaction.

Since becoming interested in the steam rally scene I had found myself fascinated with the fair organ, satisfying both my interest in things mechanical and enjoyment of music. I had to reject the thought of ever owning one. Firstly, they were far too expensive for me and also they took up quite a large amount of space which needed to be properly maintained at a suitable temperature and humidity if they are to be kept in reasonable tune. So I got to thinking about building a miniature organ. All sorts of ideas to take short cuts came to mind and one thing which I could not forget was a friend years ago having a harmonium which played rolls like a pianola. This was for sale at one time and I got in touch with the owner without delay. Too late. They had advertised it at £16 the week before and could get no takers and it had been broken up. The rolls were being used for firelighters. Hot foot I set out to rescue what I could and found the reed bank intact together with about twenty rolls, which I soon sold for the delighted owner and raised £12 for these alone. So I now at least had a useful set of reeds which would make a pleasant sound. Now, I thought, if I could get hold of an old scrap pianola and couple this to the reeds we would have an instant self-playing organ. Visualizing a suitable ornamental case there seemed to be good possibilities. Rooting around at the back of a second-hand furniture dealers I came upon just the thing. It was a 65-note pianola which had stood in the rain for some years and was clearly beyond economical repair, but all the mechanism was intact and I struck a bargain for £10. A friend brought it home on a trailer and after much prising, levering and brute force the poor old piano gave up its automata secrets and we had a heap of firewood, enough wire to defend the Thetford Battle Area and the prized pianola mechanism.

One little tiny snag arose and that was the reeds needed air pressure and the pianola mechanism needed suction. So the pneumatic requirements of the device were doubled, or so it seemed at the time. After a bit of scheming, which involved turning the mechanism upside down to make the combination more compact, the reed box was coupled to the actuating bellows so that they would lift the felt pads over the reeds to make each one sound as required. The paper drive was modified to be driven by an old gramophone motor and the roll re-wind was made to incorporate the handle and gears from an old sewing machine. This marriage proved to be entirely satisfactory.

The next major problem was to provide the air pressure. So, copying the original bellows from the pianola, two pairs were made up, one for the suction and one for air pressure. These were arranged to be driven by an electric motor through a wondrous concoction of belts, chains, cranks and levers. Which all looked splendid if you like such Heath Robinson contraptions, but the size of the whole thing was now getting somewhat out of hand. The organ was threatening to become larger than the original piano and the idea was to have a miniature instrument. Not only that, the bellows failed miserably to provide either enough suck or blow, the reeds would not tremble and the actuating mechanism would not actuate no matter how furiously the bellows bellowed. I had to think of something else and that turned out to be Mother's old vacuum cleaner. After some experiments it soon became apparent that this was so powerful that it could be made to do the sucking and blowing simultaneously! This may seem a daft statement as you cannot have one without the other, but the needs of the mechansim are quite different from the air demands of the reeds. The pianola actuating bellows need suction in little puffs whereas the reeds take air all the time they are sounding. By arranging a suitable air bleed into the suction side of the fan there was enough air to provide the pressure for the reeds. This turned out to be the complete answer and all the bellows, cranks, wheels, belts and chains were torn apart and discarded. I shall find a use for them one day! The electric fan was built into a heavy wood box and mounted on rubber and turned out to be very quiet.

Now the organ was making acceptable music it had to be surrounded with a pretty box and made to look something like a fairground instrument. One of the essentials was to provide an ornamental animated conductor. After searching for an easy way out, I had to set to with the woodcarving tools and produce a lady of my choice. She was fitted to a platform and arranged to turn from side to side with one arm holding a baton to conduct. Usually these figures are animated from the music cards or rolls to keep perfect time with the music being played. However, as there is no such provision on pianola rolls I had to find some other way. I had observed that on large organs, although the conductor is timed for each piece of music, the synchronism seems to be entirely haphazard and at the whim of the music cutter! So I decided to fit an electric motor and gearbox to drive the conductor with a random shaped cam to move the baton arm. She is switched on with the air supply, so works as soon as the music starts. The funny thing is that in the mind of the listener she appears to keep time no matter what music is being played. This is some psychological quirk of the human brain that expects her to be in time and although she is not, the brain seeks and finds the right rhythm!

The 'Goblin' organ

The organ became quite compact with the new fan and the case ornamented with split turnings and mouldings and decorated with miniature instruments and, of course, the obligatory coloured lights. It was made to pack away with a front cover which held a good supply of music rolls and has put up with quite a lot of wear and tear without suffering. What to call it? Bearing in mind the vacuum cleaner provided all the puff and suck it just had to be a Goblin!

Going back to "Duncan" the locomotive, the time had come to build a replacement and this was to be one of my biggest jobs to date. The gauge was to be 10¼ inches and if the engine was built to narrow gauge pattern with outside frames it would be quite a big engine for the track. Lines 10¼ inches apart does not seem very big does it? Come to that neither does 4 feet 8½ inches, the size of a full size railway. But it is surprising how much can be carried by those two thin steel strips. The engine was to be an 0-4-2 with outside cylinders. In order to save time the boiler was built by a firm in the Midlands who quoted a very reasonable price and delivered the goods without too much delay.

As the engine neared the state where it could run it was realised that a rally was forthcoming at the end of the season and I made every effort to get the engine running in her nakedness and then could spend the winter finishing off with all the nice touches which would change a piece of mechanics to an engine of character. So one Saturday night found the final touches being added to get steaming and about 7.00 p.m. we had a fire in the box and a short piece of track and "Edmund Hannay" was chuffing up and down for the first time. She was loaded up there and then and, still hot, was taken to the rally field and we followed with the caravan for an enjoyable weekend. I was delighted that the engine did a full two days' work and gave much pleasure to children and adults at the rally. I set to work the following winter with renewed enthusiasm to finish the engine off so that she looked the part. In the years since she has travelled the country to many events, but I am now glad that she has a permanent line at Wells-next-the-Sea and carries holiday-makers from the town to the beach all through the summer. I must say that was another great thrill, to ride behind "Edmund Hannay" pulling a full load of passengers on a regular journey. It is splendid to have a short piece of line to ride up and down or round and round, but railways *should* go somewhere.

I suppose it must have been the Soame Steam Wagon that caused the birth of the idea that led to "Buttercup" (see front cover). The Soame was a charming little steam wagon which must have been one of the most successful early steam carriages. It is simply a four-wheel wagon fitted with a coal-fired vertical boiler and a steam cylinder at each side driving a crankshaft, which then drives the back wheels by two flat belts. The steersman sits in front with the tiller and the driver is in the back tending the fire. I had always been very taken with this and used to hear my Father talk of it being built about 1890. I got to thinking how nice it would be to build one. I could not afford to put too much time into it as I had a lot of other work on hand so as usual I began to think of short cuts. I had a single cylinder engine but no boiler, so I would have to build one. Then I began to realise that I had a lovely little open crank farm petrol engine of about ½ horsepower. Suppose I used that. There would be many advantages. It would be ready for instant use. It would be much lighter so it could go behind the car in the trailer and the whole job would be simple but not lacking in character. Accordingly the little engine was cleaned up and got running. It was obvious that it had plenty of power and in good mechanical order. This little engine was built by The Frome Engineering Company and called a Hobbs. I also happened to have an old Austin 7 gearbox and I thought I could make a simple clutch with the slipping belt and jockey pulley.

I am very fortunate to have amongst my many friends a most valuable fellow with a sawmill and I very generously allow him to dump his unwanted wood here. He often has timber with nails and barbed wire in which cannot economically be sawn. So I studied the available wood and found I had a piece of elm plank which would yield two very acceptable back wheels and some pieces of oak for the front. The wheels were bushed with steel tube with lugs welded on and I started from there and built up a chassis to suit. The front axle swings just like a traction engine, but I did fit a spring into the perch bracket and this made the ride a little less shattering. The gearbox was fitted out of sight and a motorcycle chain taken to one rear wheel. Steering was by tiller, but not your conventional side-to-side action on a vertical piller, but a tiller which works fore and aft. Well, it jolly well works and there are only three components in the steering – the axle, the tiller and a link! The engine is at the rear with a handsome copper petrol tank. Driver and passenger are provided with full weather protection so long as the rain falls vertically and

Commander Francis driving 'Edmund Hannay'

there is a tail wind equal to the forward speed! The roof is provided with a hatch for extra ventilation and access to the horn. I also happened to have developed a means of making wood look very old while we were making furniture. It is not necessary that the timber be planed or have any degree of finish and I decided that our Horseless Carriage would be finished in this fashion. It has taken many people in – especially if they don't know anything about Austin gearboxes and Frome engines! When I am asked about the age I usually reply that the wood must be very old as the trees were planted quite some time ago!

The name was important and not arrived at lightly. Much thought and head scratching went into the matter, but "Buttercup" has proved very popular and successful. We get many requests during the summer for school events, fetes and rallies and are nearly always invited back again. I wish she had a mileometer. She must have clocked up quite a distance on the lawns and playing fields of Norfolk.

While on the subject of my wood antiquities, I must mention the Fog Engine. This really started many years back when the scrap lorry used to call and I actually got paid for my swarf. As usual I used to dive into the lorry to see what other less enlightened folk had thrown away and this time I came up with a handsome ornamental wheel which looked as if it had graced a mangle at some time. For the price of a few pence this prize was carefully put away in the stores for future use. It must have been ten years later that I could leave that wheel alone no longer and placed it upon the bench in a prominent place and thought about it for a few days. Yes, it would make a fine antique engine.

But what sort? Never mind, I would think of some way of making it run, but I would start on something on the lines of a grasshopper engine. I found a lovely piece of hardwood about a yard long and 3 inches thick, and turned a handsome wood column and erected this at one end. The other I fitted four columns with bearing bridges across the top to take the crankshaft so the flywheel would clear the bed. At this point calamity occurred. I dropped the flywheel! However, it's an ill wind, as they say, and looking through my stock of cast-iron pulleys I found an even better one with curved spokes. I just had to cut a piece out of the engine bed to accommodate the larger diameter, and all was well. Actually, later, when I had to match up the engine speed it was just as well the new wheel was fitted. Before going further I thought it essential that such an engine should be readily portable so a pair of sheep hurdle wheels were fixed under one end and a foot at the other. The crunch came at that point. The great decision had to be made – how would it run? It could be hot air (appropriate), it could be steam, it could be internal combustion. That, however, was more likely to result in the antiquification process being hastened to the extent of reducing the whole thing to matchwood, so in the end it was decided that steam was the stuff. I should have known it all along.

Now usually steam engines have to have some means of turning water into steam and, not wishing to have the weight and complication of a conventional boiler, I had to think of an alternative. It so happened that some years previously I had produced a steam generator which had a tremendous output of steam within a very small size and I happened to have a unit only three inches square that I knew would make all the steam needed. So with this in the back of my mind I went ahead and fitted a steam cylinder to the engine, so that the piston rod actuated the grasshopper beam. The steam admission and exhaust was worked by a pair of what had been gas taps from an old copper. These taps were driven by links taken at suitable angles from the big end and after a bit of fiddling the timing was just right. Now I could try the thing on compressed air and would you believe it, it ran beautifully, without a sound. So, further inspired, I fitted one of the heat exchange units into a furnace which was actually an old compressed gas bottle and made a chimney from a piece of car prop shaft tube that happened to be the right size. All that remained was to arrange for a pump to continuously deliver a small regular quantity of water into the generator. The heating came from a much modified Primus burner. A very old pressure gauge was fitted that looked the part, having a nice brass case and bevelled glass, and the fire was lit in a moment of great excitement and apprehension! After much dribbling of water from the drain tap the cylinder was soon hot enough to do some work and the engine began to run in a most pleasing way. Not much power, but that was not intended. It just drove itself in a quiet and dignified way. Now what to call it? After noting the steam pressure which was about 3 lb. per square inch, it was decided that as the thing was obviously running on fog it just had to be a Fog engine!

After running at one or two rallies an urge was felt that the Fog engine had to have a purpose, if only to stop people asking what it was for! What could the thing possibly drive? Many notions came to mind. The most promising at one time was a mud pie factory, but it was felt that the market was fairly limited for such a commodity – apart from the Food and Hygiene regulations – so that was shelved (only temporarily you understand). Another thought was a gramophone, but such an instrument would just have to have a large and ornamental horn, which I did not have. Numerous inquiries failed to bring one forth, so the matter had to await developments. As time went by and still nothing came to hand I had to find a way of making one. Actually a gramophone horn is a very scientifically designed thing. If the shape is not just right the sound that goes in is diminished rather than amplified. After rejecting materials like glass fibre, spun aluminium, etc., I got to thinking about some mahogany ply panels I had bought in an auction when a boat yard sold up. So I thought I would apply some rule of my best thumb and make a horn from this and if it didn't work, never mind and start again. Another motto: Do something even if it's wrong! So some suitable shapes were sketched starting with a vertical cone ending in a 45° top reflecting panel forming the mouth with various angles doubling here and there – and the darned thing worked beautifully! It has actually been heard nearly a quarter of a mile away on a still day! That was enough for me to be spurred on to build the rest of the mechanics to rotate the record. Gears were spurned as being too modern, so a simple friction drive was devised ending up with a horizontal shaft to take a pulley and belt from the engine crankshaft, without any thought of gear ratios, etc., to get the record to turn at 78 rpm. While looking for a pulley I came across a driving wheel that had come from a treadle sewing machine and this was fitted and, contrary to my original intentions, a belt was run from the engine flywheel. Steam was raised and the engine allowed to settle to the natural speed and a record put on the turntable and the tone arm lowered. Perfection! The speed was just right. As long as the engine was kept running at a steam pressure of between 3 and 4 lb. per square inch the record ran at the right speed. The engine being single acting gave a slight variation in speed, but with the addition of a friction roller driving flywheel to the turntable this was all taken care of. And what to call it? Well, what else could you call a Fog engine driven gramophone but a Phogrofone!

Ever since I remember there has been from time to time talk of fuel crises. If it isn't U-Boats it's the miners or the Arabs or the North Sea or the politicians. The thing that we are seldom short of on the East Coast is wind. So I decided on a day when I had a little time to spare that I should start to build a wind-powered generator to make us independent of those mentioned, to say nothing of the Eastern Electricity Board. Although it took only a moment to have the idea and a day to make up my mind, it took years of odd hours to complete.

Firstly, and I suppose obviously, it had to be up in the air, so I bought a

The Phogrofone

disused mast from Cecil Dawson, Norfolk's Universal Supplier. Then I thought, our forefathers controlled the speed of their sails by letting the wind through them or by feathering them to the wind in the same fashion as an aeroplane propeller works only in reverse, if you see what I mean. I also thought it would be easier to put the generator up the pole, instead of bringing the drive down to the bottom. The upshot of it all was that Richard and I, with a hand winch, got 250 lb. of alternator and 12 feet 6 inches diameter of sail up a 40-foot mast which gave us enough free juice to run all our electrical appliances when there is a minimum of 8 m.p.h. of wind – in technical terms 1,000 watts with 30 m.p.h. wind speed.

I have always nursed the ambition to build a large scale model traction engine, but there have always been other orders to fulfil and the matter had been just kept in the back of my mind with the hope that one day the chance

Wind-powered generator

would arise. And so it has. I was overjoyed to have an inquiry for just such an engine and for the past one and a half years I have had one of the most rewarding and enjoyable pieces of work to accomplish. This is a Marshall general purpose agricultural engine built to a scale of 5 inches to the foot, which makes a model about 7 feet long and will weigh just over a ton. So far I have reached the stage of fitting the crankshaft and preparing to light a real fire and having the engine running for the first time. I trust that there will be many similar thrills for this is pleasure and, like all the best things in life which cannot be bought or sold, it cannot be equalled and it has to be earned. You have to have a bit of luck too and this can depend to a great extent upon the goodwill of others. I have always valued goodwill very highly, perhaps others with advantage might do the same. A simple lesson was taught me years ago when I first started here. One evening a lorry driver walked into the workshop with a broken fuel pipe which I was pleased to weld for him so he

47

could get on his way, declining payment for such a trivial job. That man turned out to be not a lorry driver at all, but owned a fleet of vehicles and within a week he had returned and spent over £50 with me at a time when that sum was three weeks' wages! I could easily have charged him £1 for mending his fuel pipe, but do you think he would have returned?

That brings us – taking a few short cuts – up to date and you ask me what I feel about the future. I think all parents have a natural foreboding in relation to their children's prospects – I know my father did and so did his father. But I reckon that providing they can make things and do things with their hands they'll get by. Mind you, it's handy to be able to work out complicated equations, but if you can't there's clever chaps about today who invent and make little electronic calculators to do it for you. But the bright chap is the one who knows what problems he needs to solve. The other thing is I wish there weren't so many people who want to push us around, make rules, or become responsible for us. There are, of course, some people who need looking after, but I think a lot of those who do are some of the ones who spend far too much of their time and my money trying to look after me.

From my childhood days, it seems I was destined to be a loner. In some ways I look upon this with regret as I place the highest value upon the humanitarian spirit which is to be found in every one of us if only we take the trouble to look, and over the years I have looked and been amply rewarded by countless acts of kindness and generosity received from all in my path. I can only say to them, thanks for being there, I remember every one.